ATTENTION TO DETAIL

A WOMAN'S GUIDE TO PROFESSIONAL APPEARANCE AND CONDUCT

CLINTON T. GREENLEAF III
STEFANI SCHAEFER

DEDICATION

This book is dedicated to our parents:
Helen and Geof Greenleaf
Patti Schaefer
Thank you for your love, guidance and support.

2000 First Edition

ISBN: 0-9665319-3-0

Library of Congress Catalog Card Number: 99-90500

Illustrations by Danielle Sovchen

Layout by Francine Smith

Edited by Holly Strawbridge

Special Thanks to: Allyn Adams, Lee and Kaaren Arthurs, Ann Bohan,
Beth Biasiotta, Liz Connelly, Roger DePenti, Dr. Heidi Ginter, Geof, Helen
and Tim Greenleaf, Jodi Harrison, Beth Kagy, Kelly Kane, Ali Marcell, Anne
and Dusty Putnam, Kim Rose, Jennifer Sheehan and Michele Yee

Published in the United States by Greenleaf Enterprises, Cleveland, Ohio.

www.greenleafenterprises.com

This guide was written to offer options to the professional woman.
It should not be considered a guide to a strict code of dress. Following
the advice in this booklet does not guarantee any specific benefits.

TABLE OF CONTENTS

FOREWORD

The advice in this book comes from almost 60 years of training, both in life and on the job. I was an international model listed with top modeling agencies such as Ford and Wilhelmina. I was trained by "the best of the best" in the fashion world and decided to share my knowledge with thousands of young women.

I moved back to Ohio to fill my life-long dream of opening a modeling and performing arts center. In the late 1980s my daughter Stefani became my business partner and also began teaching self-improvement classes to thousands of young women. We teach how to dress, speak, greet people and how, in general, to be your best self. Together, we've groomed several Miss Ohio, Miss America and Miss USA contestants. We prepared them for a successful pageant experience, and worked on their fashion sense and clothing choices.

Stefani put all of this into play during her years in the pageant system. In 1989, she was named Ohio's Junior Miss, winning the talent award, judges' interview award, fitness award, personal appearance award and the Miss Congeniality award. That same year, she was a national fitness and appearance winner in the America's Junior Miss Program. A few years later, Stefani was first-runner up to Miss Ohio in the Miss America Scholarship pageant.

She credits her accomplishments to 28 years of preparation and learning what it takes to feel confident in the way she acts, dresses and looks. We both believe it is not only important to look your best, but it is most important to feel your best. The two go hand in hand.

Stefani is seen by thousands of viewers each day as the anchor of the top rated news and informative morning show in Cleveland. Each day she is flooded with phone calls from viewers asking where she shops for clothes and who does her hair and makeup. In this guide, Stefani and Clint share their answers, plus beauty secrets, fashion tips and tricks to help you create your own style.

Patti Schaefer

INTRODUCTION

Let's face it: in today's world, appearance and conduct matter. People are initially judged by the way they look. They earn their credibility based on how they act. Those who want to succeed take the time to look their best and act appropriately at all times.

No matter what your background may be, you can learn to look great and conduct yourself like a professional by reading this book. You will learn that attention to detail matters, not only in your career, but in all aspects of your life. The level of care reflected in your appearance and manners attracts positive attention and admiration, both of which foster confidence. Most importantly, you will begin to pay more attention to detail – a skill highly valued in the professional world.

| 1 |

WHY APPEARANCE MATTERS

You can't judge a book by its cover; everyone knows that. The problem is that people do! Our appearance is the basis for everything else we do; it is unfortunate, but a simple fact. You want to make an outstanding first impression the first time you meet someone, because you can never go back and do it again. Do it right the first time.

First, always consider where you are going. Have an interview with a bank? Dress like a banker. Have an interview with your boss about a possible promotion? Dress like you deserve that promotion. Regardless of how you want to dress, you should always dress the part. Individualism is only respected to a certain degree. Most employers will not hire someone with a pink mohawk hairdo, three eyebrow rings and visible tattoos.

This book takes the stance that although individualism and self-expressionism are important, dressing appropriately for the professional environment is necessary for success. For those of you who wish to compete in today's professional world, this book is for you. While being well dressed is not enough to ensure success, an unprofessional appearance will almost guarantee failure. The point is not to tell you what you must do or wear, but to guide you in what is considered acceptable and preferred. Even if you choose not to follow any of the suggestions, you will learn what it takes to display a professional image.

2

SHOES

Just because they are at the bottom certainly does not mean shoes are the last to be seen. Many times, it is the shoes that pull a suit or an outfit together. In fact, many of us are judged by the shoes we wear.

Make sure your shoes are clean, unscuffed and shined. If you are unsuccessful at removing all the scuffmarks, take them to a shoemaker or luggage repair shop. For just a few dollars your shoes can look like new.

Leaf through any fashion magazine and you will see different sizes of heels. For business, a two to three inch heel looks best with suits. But whatever size heel you choose, you need to make your decision based on your job duties and hazards. If a one-inch heel or even a flat shoe is best for your job, then wear it. There is nothing worse than having sore feet... or falling in heels.

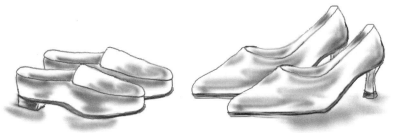

Heel thickness has varied over the decades. From thin, stilettos to chunky heels, choose what you feel comfortable wearing or what your contemporaries wear. A safe bet is to choose a classic heel, because your shoes will never go out of style. It is also a good idea to choose a heel based on your height.

Keep in mind that, in general, your shoes should match the bottom half of your clothes. But do not take this little rule to the extreme; if you are wearing a colored suit, it is not necessary to match your shoes to your suit. It might be difficult to find the same shade, and if the color is off in any way, it will clash. A woman in the business world will need shoes of various styles in black, brown, a cream or neutral color and possibly navy.

Be careful with open toes and open heels. Even with a pedicure and casual Fridays, exposing your feet is not acceptable in most conservative businesses.

There are two more rules to keep in mind concerning shoes. First, only wear light colored shoes between Memorial Day and Labor Day. Second, do not wear suede shoes into the spring: they are for fall and winter only.

STOCKINGS AND HOSIERY

In a business setting, always wear stockings. Even if you just came back from the Caribbean and have a great suntan, wear pantyhose. Pantyhose make a woman look complete and sophisticated and are required if you want to be taken seriously. To pull most outfits together, you need only the basic neutral colors: black, nude and pearl or champagne. Never try to match your pantyhose to a colored suit! Never wear red hose to match your red power suit, or green hose to match your green suit. The exception to this is if you are wearing a black suit, sheer black hose looks great. Otherwise, wear a neutral color. Also, pantyhose should always be lighter than the color of your shoes, unless you are wearing black shoes and black hose. Following this rule, when wearing black hose, always wear black shoes.

Opaque hose and tights are typically more casual and can be worn with short skirts. Sheer hose look better at night and have become the everyday choice for women living in warmer climates. Medium sheer hose can be more slimming than very sheer or opaque hose.

Although all pantyhose can run, you might get more mileage out of a more expensive pair of hose. They look natural and really compliment a woman's legs. Most brands should last several days, weeks or even longer if you care for them properly. After each use, hand wash them with a mild soap and water and hang them to dry. Avoid detergent soaps, which tend to break down the fibers. Simply swish the pantyhose in soapy water in a bathroom or kitchen sink.

Squeeze them out in a towel to remove excess water and hang them to dry on a towel rack or shower door. Do not put them in a clothes dryer, because heat destroys elastic.

For most business settings, avoid patterns; they look unprofessional. When you find a sale on good pantyhose, stock up. Keep spare pairs everywhere; in your briefcase, at your desk and even in your car. You never know when or where you'll get an irreparable run in your stockings.

To help avoid those dreaded runs, remove any hand jewelry you may be wearing and take your time when putting on pantyhose. This is when most runs occur. It is easiest to put on pantyhose while sitting down. First, gather one pantyhose leg down to the toe and slip it over your foot. Smooth the toe and heel and slowly work the hose up your leg, gently pulling out any wrinkles. Once you get to your calf area, do the same for the second leg. Stand up and work one leg at a time, pulling the hose over your thighs to your hips. Always be sure to check that you are wrinkle free.

4

BLOUSES AND SCARVES

Never underestimate the power of a white shirt. Your wardrobe should include several different white shirts. Choose a collared dress shirt, a cotton round-neck shirt and a standard blouse. White looks great with any color and compliments a power suit. Colored blouses can add to your look, but just be careful to make sure the blouse enhances your appearance and does not over-complicate it.

Scarves are a classic look that never go out of style. A scarf can really dress up an outfit, while giving a suit a totally different look. They can also be changed according to the season. For example, in early spring a black winter suit looks fresh with a bright turquoise, orange, hot pink, or green scarf. Bright splashy colors can really bring a suit to life.

Great neutral colors like black, ivory, navy blue and taupe can pull a suit together and give a subtle and classic look. Depending on the situation, and for a change, pastels and floral prints are good options. Floral prints should be worn only with solid colored suits, but have a wonderfully feminine appeal. You do not want your scarf to overpower you, just to add to your look.

Always be sure your scarf is pressed. Check the label to ensure how much heat it can withstand. If it is sensitive, you can put some fabric on top of it before pressing it. Iron it on the backside and use a low setting. Also, avoid using steam when ironing, because it can cause water spots. If you don't want to dry clean your scarves, you may check the label to see if you can hand wash them in cold water. Do not ring them dry. Simply shake them a bit and lay them out flat on a towel to dry.

There are hundreds of ways to tie scarves. When you buy one, experiment with what looks best on you. You may discover several different looks you like. And they vary from suit to suit. Here are two classic looks to help you get started.

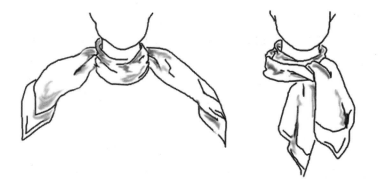

Make sure the scarf is tied or secured with a broach or pin so you are not fussing with it. Safety pins are a great way to hold a scarf in place; just be sure the entire pin is hidden.

PANTS

Although pants have not been historically accepted in business circles, many women wear them in today's professional world and look great. Depending on the type of job you have or duties you perform, pants may be appropriate in your profession.

The type of pants you choose is critical to your overall appearance. Solid colors like black, brown, navy, gray and beige look best. If you want a little variety, subtle pinstripes or a herringbone pattern is a fine option.

If you choose to wear a pantsuit, be sure the pants hang well and are not tight or formfitting. Pleats around the pockets have a nice look. Look for pants that fit snugly at the waist and hang nicely all the way to your ankles, settling on the top of your shoe. Always wear a suit jacket with your pants.

SUITS AND DRESSES

A well-tailored suit is usually best for business and will be most flattering to your body type. Years ago, women were advised to wear a men's style blazer jacket (which often meant it was baggy). This is not necessary anymore. Tailored jackets are now considered appropriate for business and will not make you look like you are hiding under a tent or wearing your father's clothes.

Women's clothing sizes are not standardized as they are for men. Therefore, you should try on several different suits so you can find out which size you are for each designer or manufacturer. You may already think you know, but in fact, you really could be wearing the wrong size. You be the judge as to which size looks best. However you may be surprised that you look much better in a suit you did not think was your size.

As a general rule in business, it is always better to be overdressed than underdressed. If you have an important meeting or an interview on a Friday, do not assume the people you are meeting have casual Fridays. You should never have to explain why you don't look the part or why you are underdressed. When invited to a black tie event, wear a cocktail dress or almost anything dressy.

If you purchase a few classic suits and separates, with a little mixing and matching your selections will evolve into multiple outfits that will stay in style for years. Your selections do not have to be the most expensive available, but should be of high quality. Look for quality suits that you will want to wear next week and next year. Other safe bets include the standard "black dress" and a nice sweater set. If you buy classic clothes, you'll have them for years and will always look great.

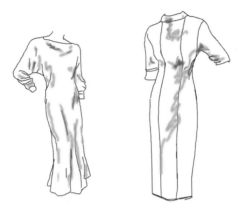

Another reason for buying designer suits is fabric quality. High quality suits often remain wrinkle free and require little maintenance. If you travel in your job or sit all day, you will quickly see this benefit. The way the material lays and hangs is also important. You don't want stiff material, or you'll feel stiff. On the other hand, some cheaper material may not hold its place and will look sloppy or too loose.

CLASSY VS. SEXY

While looking good is important, leave your sex appeal at home. Keep your standards high and people will respect you. That certainly doesn't mean you can't feel sexy or look pretty. Women are allowed to look feminine, but there is a difference between dressing sexy and dressing feminine. Being naturally sexy does not mean trying to look sexy by wearing low-cut blouses, high-cut skirts, see-through garments or night-club high heels. These elements do not belong in the business world. The key is to be attractive through class and attention to detail, not through revealing clothing.

In most professional settings, sandals and open toed shoes are inappropriate. While some sleeveless clothes are considered appropriate for "business casual," most are not professional or acceptable. The exception might be in summer and warm climates, when a sleeveless blouse or sweater can be worn under a suit coat. Don't put away your camisole! So long as it does not look too much like lingerie, it can work well with a suit. Camisoles not only look great, but they can carry you from the office into evening. Just make sure that they are not too revealing in cut or sheerness of fabric.

---- **8** ----

CLEANING YOUR CLOTHES

Getting spots on your clothes is a fact of life. What follows is a general guide on what you can do to remove certain spots from washable clothes. Keep in mind that if clothes are not washable, you should take them directly to your dry cleaner without delay.

Paper cuts often go undetected until blood appears on your clothes. As soon as you notice a blood stain, blot it with a paper towel. Then run the fabric under cold water for a few minutes. You can also use hydrogen peroxide on blood. At the earliest possible convenience, wash the fabric with color safe bleach.

Deodorant stains should be blotted with white vinegar, then the fabric washed with a color-safe bleach in the hottest water allowable (check the label for the recommended temperature). An old perspiration stain that has caused the fabric to yellow should also be blotted with white vinegar before washing. Fresh perspiration stains should be blotted with ammonia water (one teaspoon per quart). After blotting, soak the fabric in cold water, then wash it in the hottest water allowable for the fabric.

Other stains can occur during the working day. In general, most stains on washable clothes can be removed by blotting — not rubbing — then soaking the fabric under cold water. When you wash your clothes, use color-safe bleach. Coffee can be treated in this manner, as can chocolate, fruit juices and soft drinks. Ink from a ballpoint pen can be removed from fabric with hair spray. Simply spray the spot, let it soak into the fabric, then wash the garment with color-safe bleach.

In caring for your clothes, you must be willing to pay the price necessary to keep your appearance impeccable. There is no set rule for how often you must clean your dresses and suits. However, the Neighborhood Cleaning Association (an action group of Dry Cleaners) suggests cleaning after every wearing. This is probably too often for the average professional. Others say you can wait until after six wearings. As a general rule, two to three wearings is probably the most. Just make sure you feel comfortable with the cleanliness of your wardrobe.

If you choose classic styles and good fit, and properly care for your clothes, they should last for years. Read the labels carefully and follow cleaning instructions exactly. "Dry Clean Only" labels are there for a reason. Dry clean your suits after you have worn them two or three times, or as needed. When you dry clean your suits, have the skirt or pants and jacket done at the same time to ensure that the color continues to match. If one piece alone is cleaned several times, over time it may not match the jacket.

If you do not have the time or money to care for high-maintenance clothes, choose fabrics that don't need extra attention. Low-maintenance fabrics include wool knits, rayon crepes, cotton knits, synthetic blends, and almost anything machine washable. If you purchase linen, metallic, raw silk, leather or suede, be prepared to make frequent trips to the dry cleaner.

Regardless of the materials you choose, never wear something wrinkled just because you don't have time to iron it. A pressed blouse, pants or jacket is critical to a professional look.

JEWELRY AND ACCESSORIES

In the business world, keep your jewelry simple. Simple does not, however, mean non-existent. Choose no more than four accessories to wear every day. Earrings count as one and a bracelet and gold chain might be your other choices. A great look with business attire is a simple gold or silver ball earring. Buy a few different pairs in different sizes. Keep them rather small, though, as you do not want your earrings to overpower you. Pearl studs or a pearl-and-gold mix look great for daytime and nighttime. Stay away from hoop earrings in the business world. If you want to wear them, they should be small or medium in size.

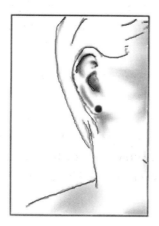

Keep rings small in number and size. One or two on each hand is appropriate. Choose a small, professional-looking watch that complements your suits. A leather or metal band is usually best. Stay away from plastic. In general, avoid fad jewelry altogether.

Another accessory to consider is your belt. A belt can complement a suit. Choose a black or brown belt with a simple gold or silver buckle.

Buy a high-quality pen for interviews and meetings. You can find one for about $10, but don't be afraid to pay for quality. A prestigious pen will really make you look good, just as a cheap pen can take away from your professional appearance. It is also advisable to carry a leather-bound portfolio for important documents and your business cards. This will enable you to carry loose papers in a professional-looking way at all times. Also, always be prepared to stitch a button on at any time. Keep an emergency kit in your purse along with an extra pair of panty hose in a small plastic bag.

Be sure you have a lint roller and use it regularly. Roll it over your clothes to pick up small pieces of lint, dirt, hair and other undesirable debris. If you have pets, you must use a lint roller before you leave the house.

Tattoos are not accessories and should not be displayed in the professional world. Finally, perfume and make-up should be used sparingly. Apply less than half of what you would typically wear on a Friday or Saturday night out. Many companies are now perfume-free. Don't let this bother you since a squeaky clean smell is always in style.

HANDBAGS

A handbag is a focal point and can lift up or ruin the look of an outfit. For businesswomen, leather is the only option, although a conservative straw bag trimmed in leather might be acceptable during the hottest summer months.

As a rule of thumb, your handbag must be relatively small and neat. If you don't have the luxury of owning many, invest in one dark and one neutral bag. Black, dark brown, and "luggage" (a dark tan) are always acceptable; white and cream are not. Navy is fine if you often wear navy, but keep in mind that a black bag goes well with a navy suit, but a navy bag does not go with a black suit.

The size and shape of your handbag are as important as the color. If you carry a briefcase, invest in a medium-sized bag with a shoulder strap. An alternative is a soft briefcase that doubles as a bag. In general, hobo bags, large sacks and backpack-style handbags are considered unprofessional, as are tiny bags, metallic colors, bags with short handles, those with sequins, glitter or embroidery and overstuffed bags. Your bag should not call attention to itself. You want to appear organized, therefore you want a unobtrusive bag that holds a wallet, glasses, phone and pens, but not much else.

Clean your leather bag regularly with saddle soap, but do not use shoe polish on it. It can rub off onto your clothes and make a huge mess. To protect the leather and color, spray the bag with a water repellent made for shoes and leather goods as soon as you buy it. When your bag starts looking weary, take it to a good shoe repair shop for a complete overhaul.

11

"BUSINESS CASUAL"

Almost everyone loves casual Fridays. But what does "casual" really mean in the workplace? Unfortunately, there is no universal definition. As a general guide, if you are at all unsure about how casual you can be, do not guess. Wear appropriate professional clothing on the first casual day and observe what your co-workers wear. Depending on your type of business, the weather, your city, and the standards of casual dressing in your office, what is considered casual may vary greatly.

Business casual usually means dress pants, a blouse and a blazer or sweater, but never jeans, sandals or tennis shoes. If your interview takes place on a Friday, do not consider this an invitation to participate in the office's casual day. You have a professional dress code to follow and many businesses still do not relax on Fridays.

Once you get the job, be sure you ask your boss or co-workers what is considered casual. Typically, slacks and a sweater set or blouse is acceptable. Once you observe the first few casual Fridays, you will get the hang of what is expected without making any serious mistakes.

When you meet with clients or make presentations, you should not dress down. You never know how the other person will be dressed, so it's always safer to look your best.

FOR THE PETITE WOMAN
(5'4" AND UNDER)

Often overlooked, this group includes millions of women. Instead of wishing you were taller, dress to add inches to your height. The idea is to dress in a way that makes you look taller and sleeker. A petite woman should always choose vertical and diagonal lines. This will make her look taller. The longer the vertical or diagonal line, the taller she will appear.

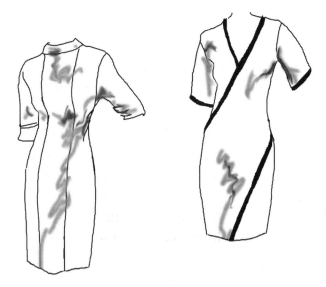

Petite women should avoid suits, dresses, blouses or sweaters with horizontal lines or that break the "north-south" axis at the waist. This creates a choppy look. When picking out sweaters, blouses, dresses or suits, be sure the line is long (up and down).

When it comes to fabric, petite women should avoid bulky and stiff fabrics and big shoulderpads. These can overpower you, and make you look like you are drowning in an outfit. Fabrics that flow well and hang softly will tend to impart a sharper look. Petite women look good in monochromatic colors, since one-color outfits appear to add height.

FOR THE TALL WOMAN (5'10" AND OVER)

Taller women have more freedom when it come to dressing, but still must follow some basic rules. Always make sure your suit fits well and that the sleeves, skirt and pant legs are long enough. Likewise, longer suit jackets and blazers are a good choice, since short jackets can look outgrown on tall women.

Because monochromatic color schemes add to the feeling of height, taller women can take advantage of color-blocking to distract from their height. Separates in coordinating colors (like a black skirt with a red jacket), belts and solids worn with patterns (a black jacket with black and white checked skirt) work well.

If you are overweight, remember that dark colors are slimming. Stay away from prints and light colors. Dress neutrally, conservatively and use a bright scarf, blouse or pin to add the color you want.

Women in business should stay away from ruffles and large, bold prints which make them look not only taller, but also bigger. Sequins and lace in the workplace are generally discouraged unless very subtle. Keep your jewelry in proportion to your size. This means that you can wear larger earrings and pins than a petite woman, but keep them conservative in size and color.

Even if you are tall, wear whatever heel size you like and feel comfortable wearing. Whereas petite women frequently wear 3-inch heels on a daily basis, most tall women do not. A 1- to 2-inch heel is acceptable with pants and skirts and looks graceful on a tall woman. Low heels are a nice alternative to flats, which are generally not worn with business attire, no matter how tall or short you are.

MIXING AND MATCHING

You need the basics to start building your wardrobe. If you purchase classic pieces, like a puzzle, they will all fit together. Start with the necessities: a black, beige, gray and navy suit, some with pants, some with skirts. Then choose a white shirt, a black turtleneck and a black shell. Next, choose black and brown leather heels. Now you can begin mixing and matching. Wear the black suit with the white blouse. For a sleeker, smarter look, wear the black turtleneck with the black suit. For a more casual look, wear the beige pants, the white shirt and the black blazer. Add a few accessories and the possibilities are endless.

When you make a purchase, ask yourself what you can wear with it. If you have a few quick answers, then buy it. Just keep in mind that the navy or black in one label may differ from the navy or black in another. To guard against this, be sure to purchase the pieces together as part of the same line.

As a rule, do not match different fabrics in the same color unless they are highly contrasting, like cashmere and chiffon. It is best to buy standard separates and suits in acceptable business fabrics like wool and its blends and rayon and its blends.

| 15 |

CLOTHES CHECKLIST

Below is a summary of the clothes and accessories you should
have in your professional wardrobe:

Clothes	Quantity	Description
Suits	4-6	At least one in black, navy, beige, also consider charcoal
Blouses	3	Plain white, black, cream
Dress Shoes	3	Black, navy, tan pumps
Belt	1	Black leather with a gold buckle
Pantyhose	10	Neutrals, pearl and black
Turtleneck	1-2	Black, white or cream
Pants	3	Basic black and the colors that match your suits
Skirt	2	Camel and gray
Raincoat	1	Black, navy or tan
Accessories		
Watch	1	High quality, gold or leather band
Overcoat	1	Professional-looking
Jewelry	Various	Necklace, bracelet and earrings
Umbrella	1	Solid color, classic style
Portfolio	1	Professional-looking
Purse	2	Black leather, for winter, lighter leather for summer

If you have these items, you will dress like a professional.
Remember, high-quality clothes and accessories will help you look
great with much less effort.

NAIL CARE

Your hands are constantly in view. That is why it is important to keep them looking their best. You do not have to have your nails done by a professional once a week. You can have wonderful nails if you care for them every few days. If you are active, then you know how difficult it is to keep nails from breaking. To help avoid chips and breaks, keep them at a practical short-to-medium length. File your nails every few days, but don't file them to a point; they should be rounded or squared slightly. Push the cuticle down with an orangewood stick only! Anything else may puncture your sensitive skin and cause an infection.

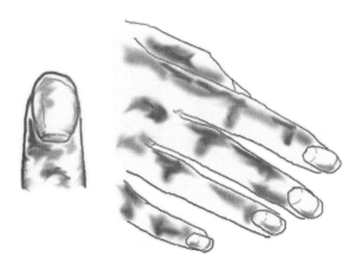

Here are some steps to a professional manicure:

---

1. Remove old polish with a cotton ball. There are several different brands of fingernail polish remover that add moisture to your nail and brands designed for all types of nails, from dry and brittle to soft and flexible nails. There is even a new gel product on the market that works wonderfully. Test them and choose what's best for you.

2. Shape your nails. Use only an emery board, since metal files are too hard on nails.

3. Wash your nails with a nailbrush. Dry your hands.

4. Apply cuticle remover and let it sit for a few minutes

5. Push back the cuticle with an orangewood stick.

6. Clean under your nails with the stick, then be sure to wash your hands.

7. Buff your nails with a nail buffer. It is important to go in the same direction. Do not use a swirl technique.

8. Apply a base coat. Wait at least two minutes and apply two thin coats of nail polish

9. After the nail polish is completely dry, apply a topcoat.

10. Apply oil or hand lotion.

A light neutral color works with everything. Choose a soft pink, taupe or sand color. These colors are great for work and will go with any color suit or outfit you choose to wear. Stay away from the newer colors like blue, black or green. Bright colors are now acceptable in many businesses. If you are not sure, play it safe and observe what your respected co-workers wear.

Having just described the process, it is important to mention that most professional manicures only cost about $10. In an attempt to save time, some businesswomen, simply have a nail care professional do the job.

PHYSICAL FITNESS

A discussion of professional appearance and conduct would be incomplete without at least mentioning the benefits of getting and staying in shape. Although there are successful professionals who succeed without being in shape, many truly successful businesswomen are in great shape. This gives them the energy and stamina they need to deal with stress and long hours. By spending the time it takes to work out and tone their bodies, they fit well into their clothes, have more energy and look like movers and shakers.

This does not mean that your career will depend on spending four hours a day in the gym. By taking about one hour every other day, you can trim down, keep your heart in shape, and have more energy. After consulting with your doctor, establish a workout plan. Decide the time of day you will work out and what you will do. Allow about an hour for your workout, plus time to cool down and shower afterwards. If you do this for a month, you will see a positive change in your overall appearance.

After you workout, be sure to drink plenty of water. A gallon a day is recommended. This may sound like a lot, but water is the most important component of your body. Refresh it, and you will stay healthy, in shape and your skin will glow.

Instead of eating three meals a day, try eating only when you are hungry, even if that means six or seven times a day. Eat just until you are no longer hungry, not until you are full. This will raise your metabolism, allowing you to burn fat at a more rapid rate.

Of course you will not be hired for a job based on your physical shape alone. Keep in mind, however, that being in good physical shape helps you feel good about yourself and, most importantly, stay healthy. If you feel good about yourself, you will exude a confidence that will be reflected in your appearance. Make it your goal to get in shape and pay attention to detail.

POSTURE

Good posture is an important part of your appearance. The way you sit, stand and walk are all interpreted by others as keys to your attitude, strength and ability to accomplish difficult tasks. "Go-getters" sit up straight, stand with style, and walk tall.

The way you carry yourself says a lot about you. If you walk into a room standing tall, you convey confidence. On the other hand, no matter how well dressed you are, if you walk hunched over, you will appear insecure and unhappy. You want to glow with self-esteem. Remember, the first impression is the key, and standing tall with confidence will put a positive spin on others' impression of you.

Stand in front a mirror and pretend you are meeting someone new. Walk or stand as though a string is lifting you up by the top of your head. Feel that string gently pulling you toward the ceiling. Pull your shoulders back, tuck your stomach in, and you are ready for success.

Don't forget this posture once you sit down. Sit in the middle of your seat, so there is about two inches from the back of your knees to the front edge of the seat. Put your knees together and cross your ankles. Your knees should be pointing slightly to the left or right, and your ankles should be tucked under the seat. This is especially important if you are wearing a skirt. You may cross your legs, but remember not to pump your top leg. Your best bet is to cross your ankles.

Remember that eye contact is more important than anything else when meeting or talking to someone. People read the way you speak and the way you listen just by watching what your eyes are doing. Look at the person with whom you are speaking and talk directly to him or her. Keep your head up, especially during an interview. Do not look down in search of answers: you will not find them in your lap. Also, if you are look away when the other person is talking, it appears as if you don't care what he or she has to say. Practice working on eye contact with family members and friends so that looking into someone's eyes becomes second nature. Remember, keep focused on the conversation and the person with whom you are conversing!

Courtesy

As a confident woman, you know that you do not need to do everything for yourself. Everyone knows you have the ability to open your own car door, sit down in your seat at a restaurant and put on your own coat. But if a male business associate initiates any of these activities, allow him to do so. If a prospective employer opens the door for you, that does not mean he is asking for a date or expects you to be subservient. It only means he is a polite person who is showing you respect. Acknowledge such acts with a smile and a thank you.

If you are being interviewed by, or are working with, a woman, especially if she is older than you are, show her common respect and courtesy. Open the door for her. If her arms are full of papers, ask if there is something you could carry. If you have to travel, be sure the most senior person has the most comfortable seat. This is usually the front seat of the car. Keep in mind that you should treat other people the way you would like to be treated.

BUSINESS ETIQUETTE

In the business world, proper etiquette is a must. Those who do not follow the rules of accepted behavior lose. Although this book is not long enough to discuss every aspect of proper etiquette, what follows is a rudimentary guide to selected important aspects.

Your demeanor – what you say and how you act in a professional setting – is extremely important to success. Obvious points include using standard English when speaking (no slang, jargon or vernacular) and avoiding emotional topics (such as religion and politics).

Keep in mind that seemingly insignificant aspects like good posture and a calm smile give the appearance of strength and a positive attitude. Studies show that people react more favorably to people with good posture and a smile. A calm smile is key, not a wide grin. A calm smile exudes dignity and power, and is proven to relax others around you. When walking with co-workers, be courteous. If you walk unusually slow or fast, adjust your speed to accommodate the others in your group. If you have a kitchen or coffee station in your office, do not be afraid to make coffee. Clean up after yourself. Spend an extra three minutes to clean up a mess or wash a dish or two, and you will generate an amazing amount of goodwill.

A business card is key to establishing yourself in the professional world. Hand them out to your friends, family, new and old acquaintances, and those who you feel may benefit you in the future. Also remember to ask for others' cards and save them. Building a large file of cards can really pay off in the future. Keep in mind, however, that it is usually inappropriate for a junior person to ask a senior person for a card. Feel free to give your card in return, but make sure the senior person initiates the process.

When you get a card, jot a few notes on the back about how you met the person, issues you discussed, and personal information that you have in common. Keep them in a centralized location like a planner or a special three ring binder with custom sheets that hold business cards. Contact the people at least once a year to keep the lines of communication open. Many people send a holiday card to everyone on their list; the minor marginal cost can help to build your professional image.

SHAKING HANDS

All it takes is three seconds, but the handshake is an important component in that very powerful first impression. The moment you are being introduced to someone, or when the prospective employer is a few feet away from you, extend your right hand. You should find a happy medium here, a firm handshake is best. There was a time when deals were sealed with a handshake. Remember, you want the person you are meeting to know that you are a solid person who can be trusted and counted on. On the flip side, do not injure the person you are meeting. You want to make the person feel good. Below are two examples of incorrect handshakes followed by the correct form.

Two Handed   *Fingers Only*

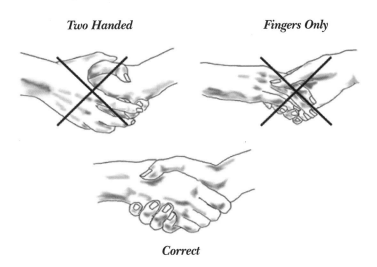

Correct

When the opportunity presents itself, square your shoulders to the person you want to greet. Smile, look them in the eye, and extend your right hand. Your fingers should be relatively close to each other, but not actually touching, and your thumb should be pointed straight up. As your hand meets the other hand, make sure you try to touch your thumb-finger web to that of the other person. Next, place your thumb on their hand, and squeeze it as if you were squeezing the ketchup out of a plastic container. You should shake gently for about three pumps, then slowly pull your hand away.

Name tags should be worn on the right breast pocket to make it easier for others to read your name when you shake their hands. This allows the eye to extend from a handshake up the arm to the nametag. At an occasion where food and drink are served, be sure to keep your drink in your left hand. Since you will shake with your right hand, you do not want it to be cold and wet from the glass. However, if you shake someone's hand and find it to be wet, cold or sweaty, do not draw attention to the condition, even in a joking manner. Act as if it were completely normal and move on. By politely ignoring it, you will help the other person feel accepted and consequently more comfortable with you.

TABLE MANNERS

Any discussion of professional conduct would be incomplete without a discussion of table manners. Many professional meetings begin, include, or conclude with a meal. While good manners may not explicitly help you, bad manners will definitely hurt you.

To get your bearings, see the illustration of a typical table setting. The simplest rule for using silverware is to work from the outside in towards the plate as the meal progresses. Your forks are on the left. If there are two, the smaller, outside fork is the salad fork, and the larger, inner one is your dinner fork. On the right, from the outside, is your soup spoon and knife with its blade facing towards the plate. A spoon or fork found above your plate is for dessert and your beverage and coffee cup will be located on the upper right corner of your table setting. Your salad plate will be on your left side with your bread plate.

As soon as you sit down at the table with others, find your napkin, unfold it and put it on your lap. Next, leave your non-dominant hand on your lap or on the edge of the table and keep it there for most of the meal. You will want to eat with your dominant hand. The only time you will use both hands is to cut your food. To cut properly, hold your fork up-side down with your non-dominant hand and your knife with your dominant hand. As soon as you have finished cutting, place the knife back on the right side of the plate or across the top of the plate, and switch your fork to your dominant hand to eat.

When eating bread, break off a small piece, butter it, and eat it. Do not butter the whole piece of bread or roll all at once. Also do not cut your food into many pieces. Simply cut off the piece you will eat, chew it well, and then cut again. Use your napkin often to clean any crumbs or food pieces from your lips. When someone asks you to pass the salt or pepper, pass the salt and pepper at the same time. Never reach across anyone's "personal space." Simply ask them to pass the item to you or pass it to them to pass further down the table.

If you get up during the meal, place the napkin on your chair. This lets the wait staff know that you will be returning soon. When you finish with a spoon, place it on the saucer under your soup dish or coffee cup, not in the bowl.

As soon as you have finished your meal, place your knife across the top of the plate, with the blade facing you. Next place your fork and other used utensils closer to the middle of the plate, tines down, and parallel to the knife. As soon as you complete your meal, use your napkin, fold it loosely, and place it on the table. If you follow these simple rules, you will greatly lessen the chances of committing a serious faux pas at a business meal.

WRITING A RÉSUMÉ

A good résumé can help you land the job of your dreams. A bad résumé can ensure that you will not get the job. What follows are some basic tips that can really help promote yourself through your résumé.

The first and most important thing is to be honest. Interviewers and human resources (HR) professionals are, by their nature, detectives. Most examine every detail with a suspicious eye and are trained to look for lies. Let's be clear: if you lie on your résumé and get caught (and you will eventually be caught), you will not get the job. Worse, you will be subsequently fired after the truth is known. When the word gets out that you are dishonest, your career will be over. It is as simple as that.

However, it is important that you not be modest. Your résumé is your best (and maybe only) chance to "toot your own horn." Tell prospective employers the good things you have done. If you have accomplished something special, talk about it. Unless you were the valedictorian, captain of the football team and National Merit Scholar, you may think you have nothing to say, but that is rarely true. Simply look back over the last few years and find the things you did that will make you valuable and desirable in the job market.

Set up a résumé in the following format. Begin with your full name, centered across the top. Use a font size slightly larger than that of the body of the résumé. If you have one address, center it below your name and include your phone number and Email address as well. If you have two addresses — for example if you are in college and live away from home — list both, justifying each against the side columns. Again, include phone and Email addresses for both.

Be careful about using your current employer's address, phone or Email address on your résumé. Unless you are certain that your current employer will not mind that you are looking for a new job, use only your home address, phone and Email. Having said that, be sure you have an answering machine or voicemail at your home. Also, remember that your potential employer will hear your message, so be certain that it is professional, short, and to the point. Try something like "Hello. You have reached <first and last name>. I'm sorry I cannot take your call now, but if you would please leave your name and telephone number, I will return your call as soon as possible."

Below your name, address, phone and Email at the top of the page, you should insert a line separating this information from the body of the résumé. Below the line, state your employment objective clearly and professionally. For example, "Objective: To obtain full-time employment with a major public accounting firm." If your actual objective is unclear, or you do not feel comfortable including one, do not use one. Keep in mind that you may change objectives to conform to each job for which you are applying.

The education section of your résumé should come next if you are right out of school. If you have been in the professional world for more than a year, you might choose to place your employment section first. Base your decision on what you think is the most revelant element of your recent past. Depending on the last level completed, you may include or exclude high school data. (If you have your graduate degree, high school information will probably not interest your employers.) If you are a recent college graduate, you probably want to include your high school name, GPA, any honors received, sports played, and activities in which you were involved. Be smart. If you did well, say so. If you were not a star student, do not say anything. Build up your strengths and avoid your weaknesses. Include the years you were in school, as well as the location (city and state) of each.

Experience or employment history usually comes next for the recent college graduate. Here you want to focus on your accomplishments, showing the jobs you have had, and how they relate to your objective, a prospective position, or your potential employer's business.

The final section can include your hobbies, interests, and involvement in outside groups and organizations. Remember that it is up to you what you include in your résumé. If you feel that the inclusion or exclusion of any item is justified and will help a potential employer make a decision in your favor, go for it. Keep your résumé condensed and to the point. If you are new to the job world, try to keep it to just one page.

INTERVIEWING

When you obtain an appointment for an interview with a prospective employer, learn about the company or organization and the job for which you are applying before the interview takes place. The Internet is a great place to start, but company newsletters, annual reports and magazine articles also can be helpful.

Try to gain a general understanding of the company, as if you were going to write a report about it. Find out who the top officers are, and if possible, their personality types. Almost without exception, the leader's personality guides the corporate culture. Study current events involving the company and its industry. You can be sure that most topics in the news will be fair game for the interviewer's questions. Current events will also give you a good base for questions to ask.

Arrive to the interview a few minutes early, in your most professional attire. Once the interview starts you will have a few moments to get a feel for the interviewer. Build rapport with him or her by sitting up straight, smiling softly, and looking him or her in the eyes when you speak. The first few minutes will create the interviewer's basic impression of you, and quite possibly, affect your chances of getting hired. Often he or she will begin the interview by discussing your résumé or an employment form designed by their company. Since the information will be familiar to you, this will help you relax. As discussed earlier in the résumé section, you must be honest. If you lie, you will be uncomfortable and stressed during the interview instead of being relaxed and freely discussing your accomplishments. Be modest but positive about your experiences and be sure to be able to explain how you overcame problems or hurdles in your life. Most interviewers now ask you for a situation in which you dealt with difficulty or failure, and what you learned in the process. If you were previously employed, the interviewer will almost always ask about your former employer. Do not take this as an invitation to complain about how horrible your experience was, or how much you hate your old boss, even if it is true. This question is designed to evaluate what kind of relationship you had with your previous employer. Be sure to be honest, but do not say that your boss hated you or you hated him or her. Try to mention the benefits of working at that job, and what you learned there that will help you in your next position.

At the end of every interview, you will be given an opportunity to ask questions. Use it. Find out what you want to know but have not been able to learn from your initial research. Having said that, there is such a thing as a stupid question in an interview situation. This can include asking how much money the position pays, the vacation policy, what does the company do, and what are your chances of getting the job. Make a point to ask something that will help you to be chosen above other candidates. Ask about a "day in the life" of the person currently in the position for which you are applying, or how the company can offer you growth, both personally and professionally. Depending on the interviewer's perceived receptivity for suggestions, you might want to use your earlier research on the company to make a suggestion for a new opportunity they might consider. Many companies appreciate this kind of initiative.

After the interview, be sure to follow up with a written thank-you letter to the interviewer or interviewers. This can take the form of a note or letter. The most important part is to thank the individual for his or her time and effort. You may also answer questions you were unable to answer during the interview, provide information to questions they asked you, or ask a question you forgot during the interview. Be sure to personalize the communication by making a reference to your interview. If you meet with more than one person, be sure to send separate thank you letters to each.

BEING ON TIME AND ORGANIZED

Not everyone finds being on time easy; some people who arrive on time have to work at it. Professionals must become masters of time. Making a point of being exactly on time is an obvious way of showing your attention to detail. People who are known for punctuality are well respected and trusted.

When arriving for a meeting, show up about one minute before the scheduled time of the meeting. You do not want to rush someone by showing up well before your set time. On the other hand, being late shows a lack of consideration. If you become unavoidably detained, call. That is what cellular or digital phones are for. Realize, however, that you should make every effort to be on time. The first time you plan to meet someone at an unfamiliar location — or if you are concerned about being late — plan on arriving 15 to 20 minutes early. You can use this extra time in your car or outside the building to deal with small administrative tasks.

The key to good organization is planning, so get a good planner. Many different styles are available, and so long as you will use it, the type does not matter. First, make sure that it allows you to plan on a daily, weekly, monthly and long-term basis. It should also have room for names, addresses and phone numbers. Some even have clear plastic sheets that can hold several business cards per page. Keep the cards you use most in these pages. For the others that you accumulate, consider getting a three-ring binder with ten-card sheets. This will allow you to keep business cards in an accessible, portable form.

BUSINESS COMMUNICATION

A business letter is an important part of professional communication. By following the proper format, you will illustrate to the reader your knowledge of business culture and how to act with attention to detail. It is best to justify all type on the left. Begin your letter with the date, followed by the name and address of the individual to whom you are writing. Next, greet the reader by the name you commonly use in conversation. If you have not met, do not use their first name. Make the letter as clear, straightforward and easy to read as possible. In the first or second sentence, convey the purpose of writing, and spend the rest of the letter discussing the point. Do your best to keep the letter to one page. Single space the type but include an extra space between paragraphs. You may or may not indent the first line of each paragraph; it is a matter of personal style. When you complete the body of the text, conclude with "Sincerely," or "Best regards." Leave a few spaces for your signature, then type your full name below.

The proper format for a business memo is constantly changing, but the following is a basic template. First, type a capitalized "MEMORANDUM" to signify the format. Next, justify all type on the left, and begin with the date, then skip a few lines, and identify the recipient by his or her complete name preceded by a "To:". Next, after a "From:," type your full name. Below the names, type "Re:" or "Subj:" and then indicate the reason for your communication. There should be three or four words describing the memo. Then write your paragraphs as separate groups, without indenting the first line. No conclusion is necessary. After you have printed it, initial it to the right of your name.

Email and voicemail are growing in popularity, and most offices use both as communicating tools. Although these formats are informal forms of communication, remember that you are a professional and need to conduct yourself as one. Begin your Emails with the proper salutation, use professional language, and keep it short. In a voicemail, greet the person, convey your point clearly, and keep the message short. If the voicemail system allows you to erase and re-record your messages if you make a mistake, take advantage of this option to sound the best you can. This may mean taking extra time to learn the system and the functions it performs.

EMAIL PRIVACY

Email is now a common form of communication in most workplaces. Many employees connect to the Internet and communicate with friends and family all over the world on company time. Some employers condone this, but others do not. Be sure to check your company's policy for personal Emails during working hours before unnecessarily endangering your job. A problem can arise when employees believe that the messages they send are private. By law, every Email you send and receive at work can be read by your employer. It is unclear how many companies actually check messages, but the important point is that the possibility exists. When using Email at work, assume that your boss and everyone else will read every word you write.

If you feel the need to send personal Emails, establish a personal account through an Internet Service Provider. There are also several free Email services on the Internet. Realize that the same laws exist for surfing the Internet and visiting the web. Any employer can get a listing of every web site you visited when using your employer's system, especially on their time, so be careful. Be sparing in your non-business use of the Internet. If you do visit sites that you would not want the entire office to know about, surf the Net away from the office.

OFFICE POLITICS

"People will talk." You have heard it before, but now at work, it is much more prevalent. When you finally get your job, you will find that office politics and the proverbial "grapevine" not only exist, but often run rampant. You must be prepared for this; expect it and accept it. Unfortunately, it is human nature.

Having said this, do not play the game. It is very easy to sit with your co-workers and complain about your boss, other co-workers, or subordinates. Do not do it. There are no good reasons to sit in on these discussions, let alone participate in them. The information — or misinformation — is harmful not only to the subjects of the discussion, but to the speaker and the listener as well. By participating, you often gather faulty information. Think about it. If you tell others how you dislike someone with whom you are usually pleasant, they will realize that they cannot trust anything you say. Rise above gossip. Stick to your work and the tasks that will help you succeed. You will be stronger for it in the end.

CONCLUSION

With the simple techniques discussed in this book, you can begin to take command of your appearance and professional demeanor. People will notice your attention to detail, and understand that you care about your appearance and professional reputation. If you keep your appearance in order and act properly, you will probably find that you are treated with respect. Most importantly, you will also feel comfortable about yourself, and be able to do your best work. Remember, attention to detail can be a great help to your career, and your life.

If you have any thoughts, ideas, suggestions, questions or comments, please send them to: Attention to Detail, Greenleaf Enterprises, P.O. Box 291, Chesterland, Ohio 44026. You can also call us at (800) 932-5420. Visit our website at www.greenleafenterprises.com or send an Email to: atd@greenleafenterprises.com.

If you would like to stay informed about seasonal trends and developments and learn more about the professional world, fill out the form in the back of the book for a FREE one year subscription to the Attention to Detail Newsletter.

ABOUT THE AUTHORS

Clint Greenleaf is Chairman and CEO of Greenleaf Enterprises, Inc. He spent three years in the United States Marine Corps ROTC program before graduating with a B.A. in economics/accounting from The College of the Holy Cross in Worcester, Massachusetts. While in college, he worked as an admissions officer interviewing high school seniors for entry into the school where he noticed a need for such a book. After graduation, he worked at Deloitte & Touche, a "Big 5" accounting firm and then passed the CPA exam.

Stefani Schaefer is a co-anchor on Cleveland's number-one-rated morning TV show, and the number-one-rated FOX network morning show in the country. She received the Ohio Governor's Choice Award in 1989 and was also Ohio's Junior Miss and Young Woman of the Year. Stefani attended Mount Union College in Alliance, Ohio, where she was an All-American Scholar and a National Collegiate Academic Honoree. She graduated a semester early with a degree in communications and journalism. She still spends one day a week helping oversee the family-owned Patti Schaefer's Performing Arts Center.

THE PRODUCTS OF
GREENLEAF ENTERPRISES

Attention to Detail:
A Gentleman's Guide to Professional Appearance and Conduct

This was the first version of *Attention to Detail* and is written for gentlemen aspiring to dress and act professionally in the business world. Each copy is only $12.95, and you get FREE shipping.

The Attention to Detail Newsletter

The Attention to Detail Newsletter is now in print! A full year is only $19.95, but as a preferred customer, we will send you a FREE one year subscription. Simply send us your name and address and we'll take care of the rest. The newsletter provides a quarterly review of topics discussed in this book, as well as reviews, financial, cooking and seasonal subjects.

Shoe-Trees

We carry the top of the line Woodlore Shoe-Trees for both men's and women's shoes. Call for our complete catalog.

Bulk Orders

If you are a business or not-for-profit institution, and are interested in a bulk purchase, please forward your request, including the quantity and product you would like to purchase.

Speaking Engagements

Clint Greenleaf and Stefani Schaefer are available for speaking engagements for your group or company. If you are interested in discussing the options for a presentation, please send your request to Greenleaf Enterprises.

For any of these products see the Order Form on the next page
or call toll-free (800) 932-5420

ORDER FORM

☐ *Attention to Detail:*
A Gentleman's Guide to Professional Appearance and Conduct

$12.95 each x _____ copies = $ _____

☐ *Attention to Detail:*
A Woman's Guide to Professional Appearance and Conduct

$12.95 each x _____ copies = $ _____

☐ **The Attention to Detail Newsletter**

One Year FREE!

Please send information on:

☐ **Shoe-Trees** ☐ **Bulk Orders** ☐ **Speaking Engagements**

Make check or money order payable to Greenleaf Enterprises with the applicable sales tax. You may also pay by Credit Card below. Send this order form and your payment to: Greenleaf Enterprises, Preferred Customer Dept., P.O. Box 291, Chesterland, Ohio 44026.

Payment: ☐ *Check* ☐ *Visa* ☐ *MC* ☐ *AmEx* ☐ *Disc*

Name _____

Address _____

City _____

State _____ *Zip Code* _____

Phone _____

Email _____

Credit Card Number _____

Exp Date _____ *Signature* _____

NOTES